MAMMAL MIGRATION

All animals migrate. A migration is any planned journey from one place to another. This book describes some interesting and extraordinary migrations ranging from a few metres to more than 2,000 kilometres.

MIGRATIONS

MAMMAL MIGRATION

Liz Oram
and
R. Robin Baker
Department of Environmental Biology
University of Manchester

YOUNG LIBRARY

First published in 1991 by
Young Library Ltd
3 The Old Brushworks
56 Pickwick Road
Corsham, Wiltshire SN13 9BX

© Copyright 1991 Young Library Ltd
All rights reserved

ISBN 1 85429 006 1

Printed and bound in Hong Kong

Contents

Introduction 6

1. Land Animals with a Fixed Home 8
Life in a Cave 9
Cave Bats 9
Migration at Sunset 10
Vampire Bats 10
Bears 12
Mice in Burrows 13
Grey Squirrels 13

2. Moving Home 15
Muskrats 15
The Mountain Sheep of Canada and Alaska 16
Scandinavian Lemmings 18
The Lemming Myth 18

3. Wanderers and Explorers 21
Wandering Gorillas 22
The Young Rabbit 23
Beavers 24
Building a Dam 24

4. Homes for Different Seasons 26
Chimpanzees 26
African Elephants 28
Bats 29
Nomads with their Herds 31
Laplanders 31
Bedouin 32
Fulani 33

5. Long-Distance Migrations 34
Caribou of the Tundra 34
The Safety of the Calving Grounds 36
Tree Bats 37
Wildebeest and Zebra 39
Crossing Rivers 40
Saiga 41
American Bison 43

Glossary 45
Bibliography 46
Picture Sources 46
Index 47

Introduction

Every year, all over the world, thousands of animals set off on long and dangerous journeys. Some, like the Hoary bat of North America, fly well over 1,000 kilometres across oceans. Others, like the Caribou reindeer that live in Canada, trudge hundreds of kilometres across frozen landscapes.

Animals have been making journeys for millions of years. The journeys they make are called 'migrations'. Animals that make migrations are called 'migrants'.

Some migrants, like the caribou, get together in massive herds when they migrate. A herd of caribou can contain thousands of animals. The older members of a herd will have migrated many times before. Their job is to lead the younger members. The Hoary bat, though, migrates entirely on its own. However, not all migrations are as long and

A herd of zebra galloping magnificently across the African plain. Within hours of being born zebra must be able to keep up with the herd.

spectacular as those of Hoary bats and caribou.

Many animals make quite short migrations. Gorillas, for example, make lots of short journeys throughout the day. They move from one feeding ground to the next, and hardly ever sleep in the same place two nights in a row.

Not all animals migrate during the daytime. Many do their journeying under the cover of darkness. Lemmings, though, are in such a hurry to get where they are going that they travel during both the day and the night.

In this book you can read about the migrations of many different kinds of animals, as well as those of reindeer, bats, gorillas and lemmings.

Most bat migrations take place at night. Bats find their way by uttering sounds, and listening to the echoes bouncing back from trees, buildings, and even insects.

1 Land Animals with a Fixed Home

All over the world there are animals living in fixed homes. A fixed home might be a hole in the ground, or a cave. Some animals, like the Grey squirrel, build homes for themselves. Most animals try to spend as much time as possible in their homes. Here they are safe and warm. However, every so often, all animals have to leave their homes and go out on journeys. Most of these journeys are quite short and are made to find food and other things. For example, as well as going out to look for food, a mouse may also collect soft leaves for its bed. In this chapter we are going to look at the different types of homes in which animals live, and the journeys they make.

Coyotes used to inhabit only western North America. In the last century they have spread to the east coast and as far north as Alaska.

Life in a Cave

Pet dogs and cats share houses with people. Wild cats and dogs, however, like the cougars and coyotes of North America, often live in caves. There are many types of animal that make their homes in caves. A cave shelters the animal from the wind and rain. Also, caves never get too cold or hot. Animals that live in caves usually make only short journeys. However, they are still tiny migrations of a sort. First we shall look at the Cave bat and the Grizzly bear.

Bats are night-flying creatures. They like to spend the day sleeping in their caves. They hang upside-down from the roof by their toes.

Cave Bats

Bats are mammals. They are covered with hair and give birth to live babies. The babies feed on their mothers' milk. Many people think bats are very ugly. Some have strange-looking fleshy growths around their nose and mouth. Bats also have a very odd way of resting. They hang upside down from the roof of the cave. They never fall away from the roof, even when they are fast asleep.

Bats hunt for their food at night. They rarely come out of their caves during the day. Most cave bats eat insects that fly at night, like moths. As soon as it is dark, they set off in search of food. Although they do not have especially good eyesight, bats rarely bump into anything as they fly around at night.

While they are in flight, bats make special sounds in their throat and mouth. The sounds are very high pitched and cannot be heard by humans. The bat sends the sounds in a particular direction. The fleshy growths around its mouth and nose help the bat to do this. The sounds then bounce off solid things like rocks, trees, or even other bats. By listening to the sounds as they bounce back, the bat can tell whether there is anything in the way. If there is, the bat can avoid it. This is called echo-location.

Migration at Sunset

Bats often sleep right at the back of their caves. Here they are well out of the reach of other animals. Some large caves are homes to millions of bats. They hang together on rocky ledges as close as sardines in a tin. Every night, just before the sun goes down, they leave the cave to feed. From a distance the thousands of bats look like a dense smoke swirling out of the cave. Sometimes it takes

Unlike the vampire of folk tales, vampire bats are less than 10 centimetres long. They feed on the blood of animals, including humans.

as long as half an hour for all the bats to make their exit.

Once they have left their cave, the bats may fly several kilometres before they start to hunt for food. Bats use echo-location to help them catch their food. The sounds bounce back off moths and other insects. As soon as they have eaten enough, the bats set off back home.

Vampire Bats

Not all bats feed on insects. Some bats, called Fruit bats, eat fruit. Others, called Vampire bats, feed on the blood of other animals. They will attack birds, deer, cattle, and

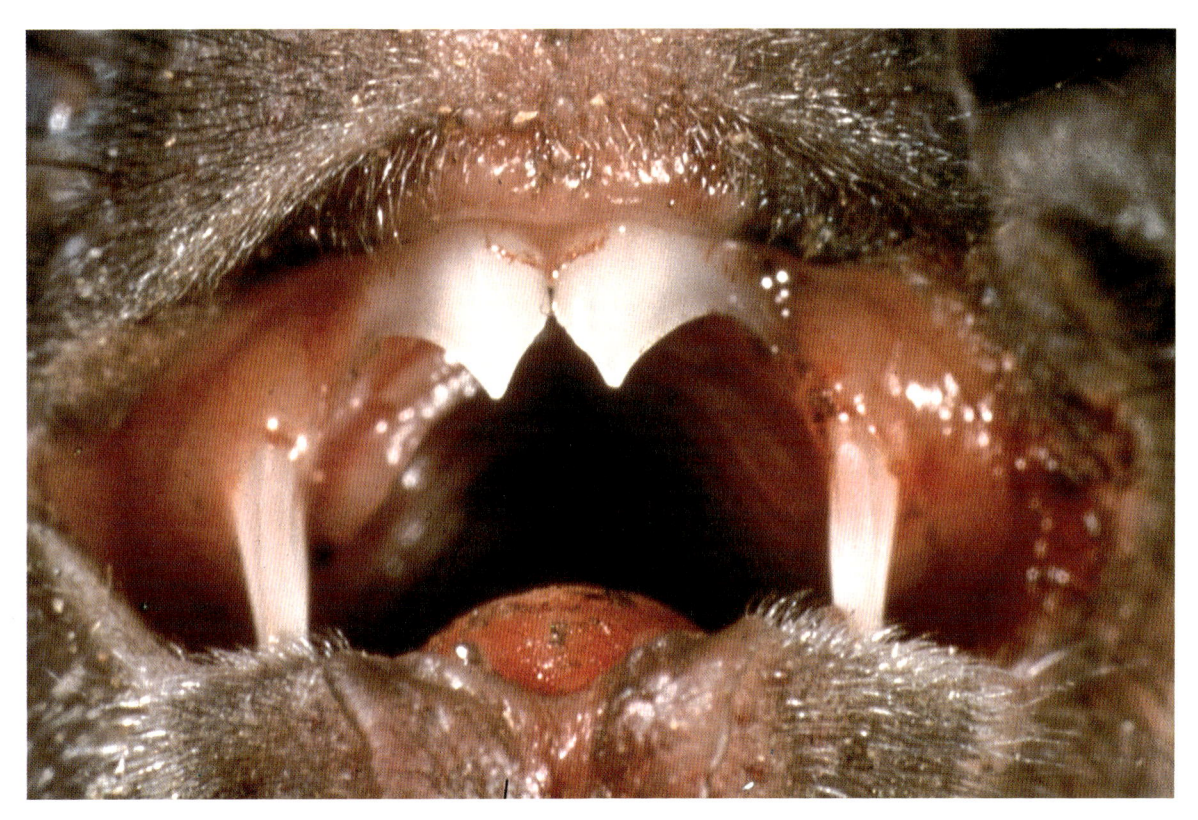

With its needle-sharp teeth the vampire bat makes a quick and shallow bite. It then drinks the blood without waking its victim.

sometimes even humans. As you probably know, vampire bats have been the subject of many a bloodthirsty horror film.

Vampire bats live only in Central and South America. They live in colonies that contain about a hundred bats. Most vampire bats spend the day sleeping in caves. Some sleep in hollow trees. At night the bats fly out in search of a victim. They do not usually have to travel more than a few kilometres before they find food.

Vampire bats usually attack cattle. They usually bite the cattle on the neck, shoulder or leg. Usually, humans are bitten by vampire bats only if they sleep outside in the open. The vampire bat's favourite place for biting people is the big toe! However, this is not as painful as you might think. Most victims do not know they have been bitten at all until they wake up in the morning with a very sore toe!

Vampire bats have two very sharp teeth at the front of their mouths. A hungry bat sinks these two teeth into the skin of its sleeping victim. As the blood flows out of the wound, the vampire licks it up, just like a greedy cat lapping up cream. There is a special chemical in the vampire's saliva which stops the blood from clotting.

As soon as the vampire has lapped its fill, it makes its way home.

Bears

Grizzly bears are found in western North America. They are large, heavy animals that lumber along on all fours. When a grizzly bear stands on its hind legs it is taller than a man. However, despite their size, grizzlies are quite fast runners. They run swiftly and can reach speeds of up to 20 km an hour. As well as eating leaves, berries, and insects, grizzlies will also catch and eat small mammals whenever they can.

During the winter months, the ground where grizzlies live is covered with snow and the weather is cold. Grizzlies do not like the cold, so they retire to their caves. They spend the whole winter in a state similar to a deep sleep. This type of behaviour is called 'hibernation'.

The bears wake up from time to time but they do not go outside. Female bears give birth to a cub in the middle of winter. The cub stays in the warm cave and feeds on its mother's milk until spring.

When spring comes, the bears begin to venture out from their caves. Most of the migrations they make are to find food. The bears know the surrounding countryside very well. Usually a bear has to travel only about a kilometre before it finds a meal. However, about once a year, some bears will make a longer migration in order to feed off their favourite food. This favourite food is a fish called salmon. At certain times of the year, the rivers are full of salmon. They are looking for a place to lay their eggs. You can read about salmon and their migrations in another book called *Migration in the Sea*.

Grizzly bears know just when the salmon are migrating in their local river. Some grizzlies will walk 20 km or more in order to go fishing. They wade in the river and catch the salmon in their heavy paws. They may stay at the river and feast on fish for many days. However, as soon as the salmon have gone, the bears always return to their caves.

Mice in Burrows

Caves are too big for some animals to feel comfortable in. Many animals prefer to dig holes for themselves in the ground. These holes are usually called burrows or dens.

Mice dig very narrow burrows. The tiny entrance stops animals such as dogs, cats, and stoats entering the burrow.

Mice usually make only very short journeys. Nearly all these journeys are made to find food. Most mice feed within a few metres of their burrow entrance. Sometimes, though, a mouse will run for a kilometre or more to feed in a special place. This place might be a field of corn or potatoes. The mouse scurries home as soon as it has finished eating. Many mice have special tracks, just like roads, that they have worn down as they run to and from their favourite eating places.

Grizzly bears are not great travellers. But when salmon are migrating upriver the grizzly will travel 20 kilometres or more, and spend days feasting in the water.

Grey Squirrels

Grey squirrels are timid creatures, but strangely they often live quite close to people. Some live in parks or even gardens. Perhaps you have watched one scamper nervously across a stretch of grass before disappearing up a nearby tree.

Originally, Grey squirrels were found only in the eastern United States. Then a few were brought to Britain. After being released into the wild to breed, they soon spread to most parts of Britain.

Squirrels spend most of their time in trees, jumping from branch to branch. They even build their homes high up in trees. Here they are safe from the jaws and claws of foxes, dogs, and cats. A squirrel's home is called a 'drey'. Dreys look like big, untidy birds' nests. Unlike nests, though, a drey has a roof. The roof keeps the squirrel and its young warm and dry.

The squirrel builds its drey by loosely weaving together lots of

Squirrels do not travel further than they need to. They avoid journeys by collecting food in autumn and storing it for the winter.

twigs. Most dreys are very secure. They are hardly ever blown down in strong winds. Squirrels do not like to venture far from their dreys. A hungry squirrel will travel only a few hundred metres in search of food. Nuts are their favourite food, particularly acorns and hazelnuts.

In autumn, when there are lots of acorns and hazelnuts around, squirrels collect as many as they can. Instead of eating them all, they bury them in the ground near to their dreys. Squirrels are very good at remembering where they have hidden their nuts. Whenever they feel hungry in winter, they go and dig up a nut and eat it.

2 Moving Home

In the last chapter we looked at a few animals that live in a fixed home. Their migrations were usually quite short. Most of them were to look for food. Some made tiny migrations in order to collect material for their homes. The grey squirrel, for example, went out to collect twigs for its drey.

Some animals stay in the same home all their lives. Others are often forced to find new homes. Perhaps the food supply near to where they live runs out. Perhaps their home is destroyed by bad weather — a storm perhaps, or even a flood. In this chapter we are going to look at some animals that are frequently forced to find new homes. We shall start with the Muskrat.

Muskrats

Muskrats used to live only in North America. However, not too long ago, a few were caught and taken across to Europe. They were released into the wild to breed.

Muskrats look like oversized rats. Most grow to a length of about 30 cm. They make homes in wet places, and like to spend much of their time swimming. Marshes, streams, rivers, and ponds are all good places for a muskrat to make its home. What does a muskrat's home look like? They dig burrows in the banks by the side of water. They leave their burrows only when they are hungry.

Sometimes, if it does not rain for a long time, the wet places where muskrats make their homes dry up. This means that their food disappears. The green plants die, the fish swim off to deeper waters, and the frogs hop away. When this happens, the muskrat has to leave its home and build a new one in a watery place that has not dried up.

It can take a muskrat a long time to find a new home. Sometimes they

A muskrat carries a mouthful of nesting material to its new home burrowed out of the river bank.

A group of rams keep careful watch from their vantage point. Only when certain there is no danger will they migrate to another mountain.

have to travel as far as 35 km from their old home. During such long explorations the muskrats are easy prey to hawks, owls, foxes, and stoats. The homeless muskrat has to be very alert and watchful.

Sometimes, if a muskrat is having no luck in finding a suitable place to dig a new burrow, it will steal one. Muskrats often take over the burrows of mice and dig them out larger. The mice then have to search for a new home themselves.

The Mountain Sheep of Canada and Alaska

Wild sheep live in flocks, just like the sheep in a farmer's field. They like to live high up on hills and mountains. Here they are fairly safe from their worst enemy, the wolf.

Wild sheep of north-western Canada and Alaska sleep out in the open on the ground. They feed on grass. However, the grass grows only very slowly. Sometimes, the supply of grass runs out completely. When this happens, the sheep have to migrate to another mountain where there is a fresh supply of grass. In order to reach the next mountain the sheep might travel many kilometres, and they will have to cross valleys.

Crossing a valley between snow-bound peaks can be a dangerous journey for a sheep. There may be rivers to ford, and they must keep out of the way of hungry wolves. The sheep actually plan their migration. Instead of setting off straight away down the mountain side, they spend a few days quietly sitting and feeding around a good rocky look-out point. From this vantage point they can see and hear what is happening in the valley below. They look out for the movements of wolves in the valley. Eventually, they work out the most wolf-free route across to the other side. Then they run down the mountainside, across the valley, and trot up the other side to fresh food and safety.

Many wild sheep live on mountains. They climb high above the treeline even when the slopes are rocky and snow-covered.

Scandinavian Lemmings

The lemming looks a bit like a large hamster. Perhaps you have seen hamsters kept in cages as pets. Scandinavian lemmings live on the tops of mountains in Sweden and Norway. Mountain tops are very cold and windy places to live. Tall plants are unable to grow there. The only plants which do grow on mountain tops are all very short and lie close to the ground.

Lemmings live in burrows that they dig in the mountain tundra. On summer nights they creep out of their burrows to feed on the surrounding plants. In winter, though, the ground is covered with snow. The lemmings have to tunnel their way along under the snow, feeding as they go. Lemmings themselves are the favourite food of lots of animals, especially Snowy owls and Arctic foxes.

Lemmings have lots of babies each year. If all the babies born in one year survived, the mountain could be overcrowded with lemmings. In most years the owls and foxes catch and eat enough lemmings to keep their numbers just right. In some years, though, the owls and foxes do not catch enough lemmings. When this happens the mountain top really is overrun with lemmings. They eat so much that

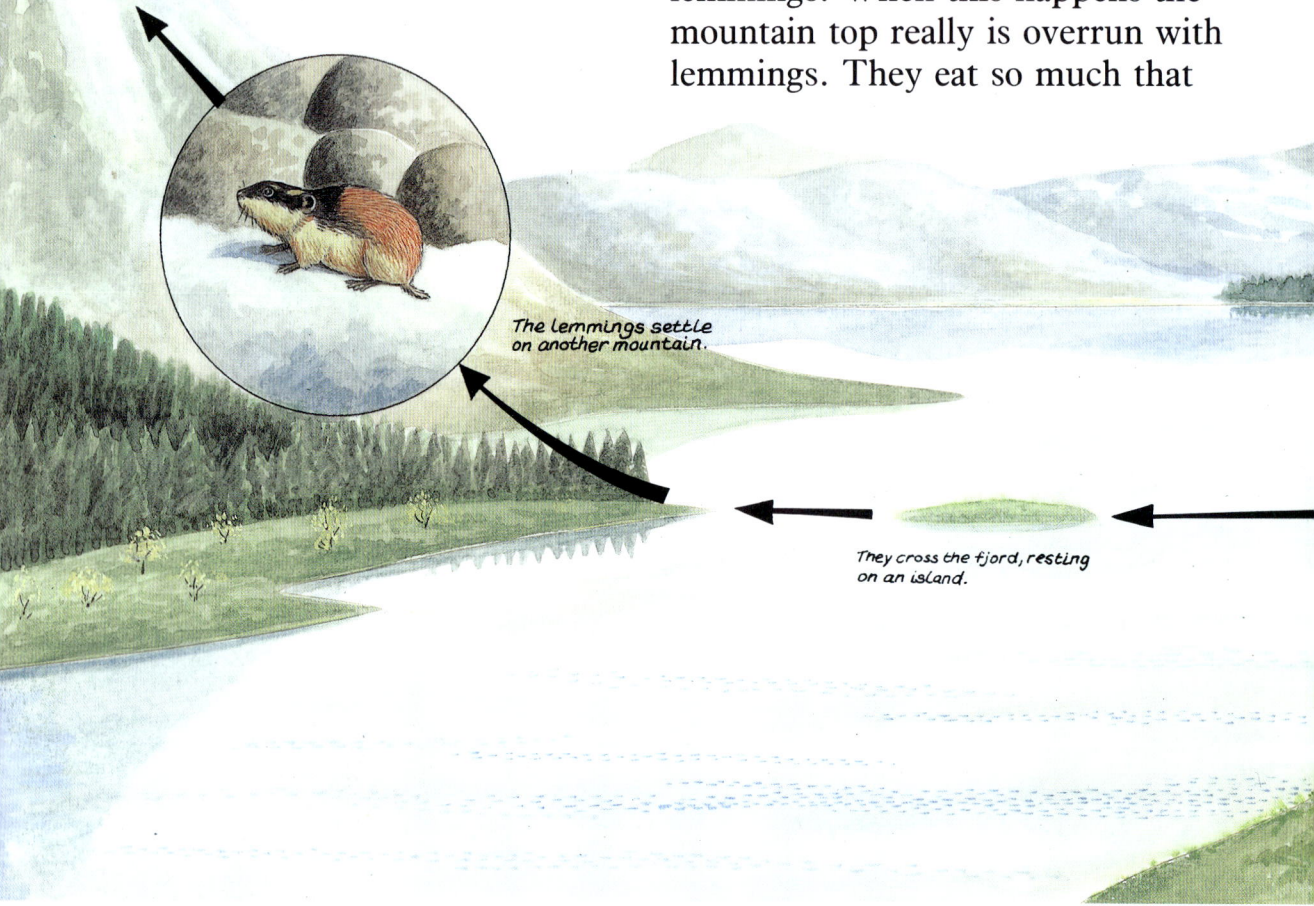

The lemmings settle on another mountain.

They cross the fjord, resting on an island.

soon there is no food left. Many of them die of starvation. Those that do survive have no choice but to migrate to another mountain top.

Sometimes thousands of lemmings are forced to leave their mountain top homes. They are in such a hurry to find a new home that they actually run when they migrate. They travel both by day and night.

For the lemmings, the journey from one mountain top to another is a long one. It is also very dangerous. Many of the migrants are caught by owls and foxes long before they reach the bottom of the mountain. For those that do make it all the way down the mountain side and into the valley, other dangers are waiting.

In all valley bottoms there is water, usually a river. In Norway and Sweden many of the rivers are very wide and form lakes. Near the coast, the sea water comes into the valleys to form lakes called 'fjords'. The lemmings have to swim across the water if they are to reach the mountain on the other side.

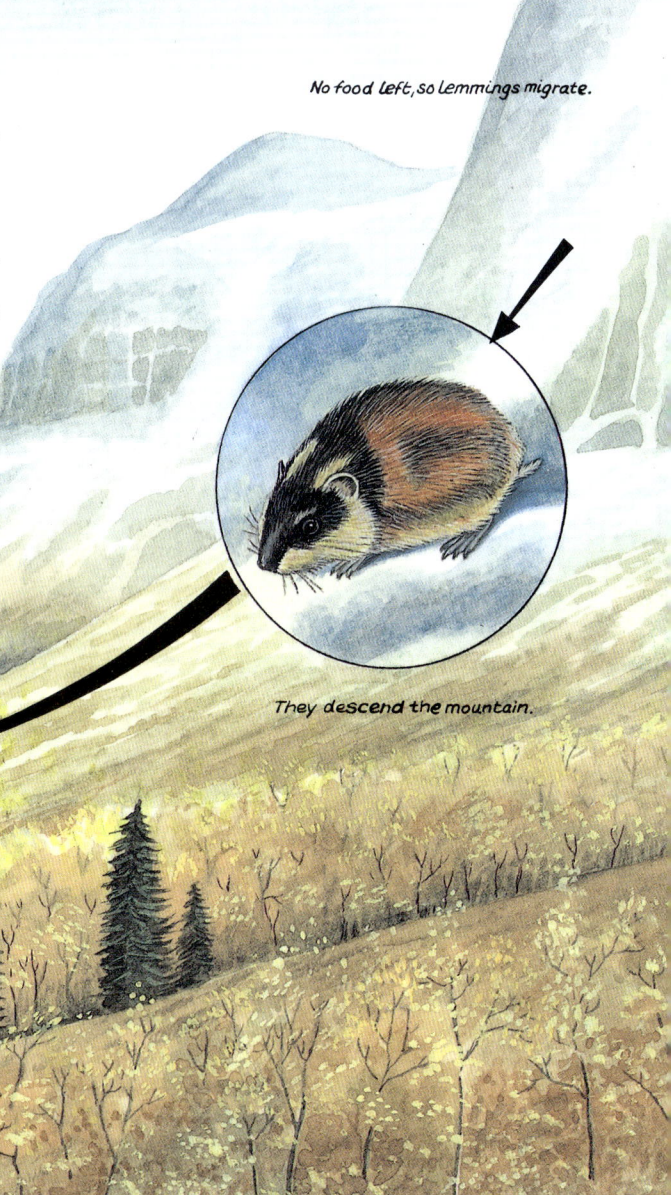

No food left, so lemmings migrate.

They descend the mountain.

They wait for good weather.

Lemmings are very clever animals. Although they are quite good swimmers, they do not like to spend too long in water. So, as they are running down the mountainside, they look out for each view of the valley below. Whenever they catch a glimpse of the lake in the valley bottom, they head for its narrowest point.

The lemmings like the water to be very calm. They also want to see where they are going. Sometimes they like to rest on islands in the middle of the lake. However, if it is foggy, the lemmings cannot see these islands or the other side of the lake. So they wait until the weather is calm and still before setting off across the water.

A few lemmings always drown, even if the water is calm and still. Most, though, manage to reach the other shore and set off up the mountain side.

Those that reach the mountain top begin to look for suitable places to dig their new home burrows.

The Lemming Myth

Sometimes the lemmings have to wait several days at the lakeside for good weather. While they wait, other lemmings keep on arriving at the crossing place. By now the lemmings are hungry. They look for food at the lakeside. However, with so many of them, soon there is no food left. More and more migrants arrive at the crossing point.

When there are too many lemmings for the food supply, they migrate. Vast numbers travel day and night.

Sometimes the lemmings get so desperate for food that they set off across the lake, even though the weather is not right. When this happens, many drown.

For centuries the people of Scandinavia watched the lemmings running down mountainsides and crossing lakes. They also noticed that sometimes many of them drowned. To try to explain what they were seeing, the Scandinavians invented a story. The story said that, every so often, the lemmings on the mountain tops developed a mad urge to kill themselves. So they ran down the mountains and threw themselves into the water to drown. However, we now know that this story is a myth. The lemmings are really migrants, and are trying very hard to stay alive.

3 Wanderers and Explorers

Many animals do not have a fixed home. In the last chapter we looked at the mountain sheep of Canada. Mountain sheep have no fixed home. At night, instead of going back to a cave or burrow to sleep, the sheep just beds down on the ground wherever it happens to be. This type of home is known as a 'home range'. The sheep wanders around in its home range, and only leaves if it is forced to.

In this chapter we shall look at another animal that has a home range — the Gorilla. Just like the sheep, the gorilla makes tiny migrations within its home range.

We are also going to see how animals look for a good place in which to make their homes. Nearly all mammals do this. We are going to follow a young rabbit as he

Gorillas do not have a fixed home. They migrate around their home range, and rarely stay more than a single night in one place.

searches for his first home. We shall also look at how an adult beaver explores for a new home for his family.

Wandering Gorillas

The gorilla is the largest of all the apes. Gorillas live in the huge forests of Africa. Despite their ferocious appearance, they are not man-eaters. In fact, gorillas do not eat meat at all. They spend most of their time peacefully consuming large amounts of tree bark, leaves, roots, and fruit.

Gorillas live in family groups. Each family group contains several females and their babies, but only one powerful male. This male is the father of all the young gorillas. Each family has its own home range within the forest. Sometimes, the home ranges of different families overlap. Gorillas do not usually mind this, and are quite happy to share parts of their home range. If two families meet in the same home range, they just sit around and stare at each other. In the end, each group peacefully wanders off back into the forest.

Gorillas know all the trees in their home range very well. They know when each tree will have fruit. They also know when the leaves of each tree are at their tenderest. When they have taken the most tender bark and leaves from a tree, they move on to another one. They know exactly how long to leave each tree to

A young female gorilla in the mountain forest of Rwanda. She is busy making the treetop bed in which she will spend the night.

recover before going back to it.

Gorilla families spend their time wandering from one part of their home range to another. Their home range can be many kilometres square. Gorillas rarely sleep in the same place two nights in a row. They sleep high up in trees, well out of the way of hungry, prowling leopards. Every night, before going to sleep, each gorilla has to make its bed. They make their beds by weaving together branches and twigs into a sort of basket shape.

The Young Rabbit

There are many different types of rabbit living all over the world. At first, the most common type of rabbit lived only in Europe. However, it has now been taken to places as far away as Australia.

The European rabbit lives in big groups. Each group digs a long, complicated system of burrows underground. These burrow systems are called 'warrens'. The rabbits spend a lot of time in their burrows. Here they are safe and warm. The females give birth to their young deep inside the warren, well out of the way of any foxes.

Not every rabbit can stay in the burrow where it is born. To avoid overcrowing, some must migrate and look for a new home.

Two or three times a day the rabbits come out of their warren to feed. They do not go far. Often they feed on the grass and plants just outside the warren. The young rabbits come outside to feed as soon as they are too big to live on their mothers' milk. Within just a few weeks, they are ready to become parents themselves. First, however, many of them have to find a new place to live.

Some young rabbits stay and live in the same warren as their mother.

Only a few rabbits can do this, though. If lots of them stayed in the warren it would soon become overcrowded. Most of the rabbits have to leave. Many will join another, less crowded, warren. A few may start entirely new warrens.

The young rabbit finds a new home by going off on explorations. Explorations are a type of migration. Every evening, just before dark, the rabbit sets off from its burrow. It travels quite fast, loping along at a steady speed. Every so often it will stop, sniff the air and look around. It may stand up on its hind legs to get a better view.

Each night the rabbit travels several kilometres. As well as visiting other warrens, it is testing the soil to find one that is right for digging. After an hour or so of exploration it returns home. The young rabbit explores a different area, each night. Sometimes it goes back to places to have a second look.

After a week or so of nightly exploration, it makes its decision. One night it doesn't come back. It has started life in its new home.

Beavers

It is not only young animals which go exploring for a new 'first' home. Sometimes even fully grown animals go looking for a new home. One of the most interesting explorers is the beaver.

This animal used to live all across North America, northern Europe, and northern Asia. However, for hundreds of years the beaver was hunted for its fur. It is now a rare animal, and has almost disappeared from many areas. Beavers look very much like large rats except that they have much thicker fur and webbed feet. They also have big flat tails.

The beaver uses wood to build its home. A beaver's home is called a 'lodge'. They build their lodges in the middle of shallow lakes and ponds.

Building a Dam

Beavers can make their own ponds and lakes by building a dam across a river. After a few years the dam and lodge become old and rickety. One summer the male will set off in search of a new site for his dam and lodge. He leaves his family, and may explore places as far away as 10 km. Eventually, the male beaver returns to his family. If he has found a good new place, he leads his family there. Then they busily build a new dam and lodge in time to have somewhere warm and safe before winter.

After arriving at the new site, the beaver family begin to build their new home. First, they start to chop down trees. They do this by chewing at the bottom of the tree trunks. When enough of the trunk has been chewed through, the tree falls over. The beavers know exactly how to chew each trunk so that it falls across the water in just the right place.

As each tree falls into the river, the water flows more and more slowly. At this point the beavers start chopping down trees further upstream. These float on the new lake and the beavers tow them to their dam. The dam grows, and the lake gets deeper and deeper. When the lake is deep enough, they start to build the lodge.

Just like the dam, the lodge is also made from chopped-down trees and branches. The wood is wedged into the bottom of the lake. As the animals add more and more branches, the pile grows above the level of the water. The entrance to the lodge is made in the part of the lodge that is still under water. The beavers can swim into their lodge and then climb up into the dry area. Here they build a sort of platform where they can rest and sleep.

Inside their lodge the beavers are protected from the wind, rain and snow. They are also safe from foxes, wolves, and other predators. The beaver has to work very hard to build its lodge but its reward is a safe and comfortable place to live.

A beaver gnaws down trees to make a dam across the river. A lake will form behind the dam. In that lake he will build a new home.

4 Homes for Different Seasons

In this chapter we are going to look at a few animals that have different homes at different times of the year.

Most of you will know the seasons of the year as spring, summer, autumn, and winter. Winters are cold and wet. The days are short and the nights are long. Summers are hot and dry with long days and short nights. Some animals have separate homes for winter and summer. However, some animals have a third home where they live in the spring. These animals migrate between their three separate homes.

In some parts of the world the seasons are different. For example, in the tropics, it is hot all the year round. The tropics is a band around the middle of the earth about 5,500 km wide. Within the tropics there are large areas of grassland. In these grassland areas all the rain falls during a two or three month period. This time of the year is known as the 'wet season'. Three or four months after the wet season ends, all the ground is dry. Sometimes it is so dry that many of the rivers dry up completely. This time of the year is known as the 'dry season'. Some animals, like the African elephant, have one home range for the wet season and another for the dry season. The elephants migrate between their two homes. However, first we shall look at another animal which sometimes has two home ranges — the chimpanzee.

Chimpanzees

Chimpanzees are a type of ape. They live on the edge of the huge African forests. Just like gorillas, chimpanzees live in groups. Each group has its own home range within the forest. The chimps wander through their home range looking for food and making sure that no other group intrudes. Chimpanzees are much more aggressive than gorillas and will sometimes kill an intruder.

Sometimes a chimp group decides that its home range is too small. It tries to take over as much of a neighbouring home range as possible. Chimps often invade neighbouring home ranges in this way. Large and powerful groups may kill off all their neighbours and then take over the spare land.

Unlike gorillas, chimpanzees do not live in family groups. A group of chimps can be quite large, much larger than the size of one family. Some groups contain as many as 40

Chimpanzees move daily around their home range in the forest. Unlike gorillas, they might have one home range for the wet season and a separate one for the dry season.

individual chimps. The males, females, and young are all mixed up together. The young chimpanzees have no idea which male in the group is their father.

Chimpanzees eat more fruit than gorillas. They also eat other animals. As well as insects and birds' eggs, chimps often catch and eat monkeys. Chimps have also been known to take and eat unguarded human babies. They are cunning hunters, and often work together to catch prey. One or two will hide in ambush while a few others chase a small antelope or monkey towards them. As soon as the frightened creature is close enough, the waiting chimps leap out into the open and attack it.

After the wet season, there is lots of fruit on the trees. The chimpanzee groups take life easy, moving from one fruit tree to another. However, in the dry season, fruit becomes more scarce. Each group of chimps splits up into smaller groups of three or four. These small groups then scatter throughout the forest in search of fruit. When they find fruit, the chimps start jumping up and down and making a lot of noise. This lets the other groups know where the food has been found. The other groups then come and the food is shared.

In some places, different parts of the forest have fruit in the different seasons. Some groups of chimpanzees have one home range in the wet season and another home range in the dry season. These different home ranges may be several kilometres apart. Twice a year, the group sets off together to migrate to its other home.

African Elephants

Elephants live in groups called herds. Most elephant herds contain only mothers and their young. However, sometimes a large adult male will join the herd in order to spend time with the females.

Elephants eat leaves and roots. They use their tusks to dig and pull roots up out of the ground. Elephants especially love to eat the young tender shoots of trees. To get at these delicious shoots, the elephant first has to break off any older branches that may be in the way. Sometimes elephants will push over whole trees with their heads. Elephants are very strong animals.

Most of the elephants in Africa live in 'scrubby' forests. In such forests there are enough trees and leaves to keep the elephants well fed throughout both the wet and the dry season. However, for the elephants that live on the slopes of Mount

In the dry season, East African elephants seek greener vegetation on Mount Kenya's slopes.

Kenya in East Africa, life is not so easy. Here the elephants need to have two separate homes, one for the dry and another for the wet season. The elephants migrate between these two homes. During the dry season, they migrate up the slopes to homes higher up the mountain. This is because the dry season is never as hot and dry high up a mountain. The leaves stay green and fresh for a lot longer.

In the wet season, the elephants migrate back down the mountainside. Altogether, the elephants may travel as far as 15 kilometres between their two homes.

Elephants will travel long distances for seasonal foods. Here a herd of cows with their young enjoy a rest at a waterhole.

Bats

We have already seen, in Chapter 1, how bats like to live in caves. Some bats live in the same cave all year round. These bats have only one home. However, not all bats are like this. Some have two homes, one for summer and one for winter.

In spring, the bats leave their winter cave. The males and females migrate separately. Each male goes off either on its own or with a few other males. They will make their summer home in the roof of a house, perhaps, or a hollow tree.

In summer the females have their babies. Most bats have only one baby each year. This is because when the baby is first born, it cannot be left on its own, even for a very

Thousands of cave bats will share a cave all winter. In spring males and females depart separately to a second home perhaps far away.

short time. So the mother carries her baby around with her. The baby clings to its mother's fur as she flies around. It would be very difficult for the mother to carry two babies around in this way. However, soon the baby is old enough to be left hanging up at home while the mother goes out to catch insects. The female has a very busy time indeed. As well as catching insects for herself, she also has to produce enough milk to feed her baby.

For the summertime, female bats get together in groups called 'nursery colonies'. Most of these colonies contain no more than about 200 bats. They need to make their summer home in a place big enough to house the whole colony. Female colonies often spend the summer in small caves, or in the roofs of large, derelict houses.

Female bats help each other to raise their babies. They arrange a sort of baby-sitting rota. This makes sure that at least one mother is always left at home to guard the babies. Sometimes, before they can fly, young bats fall from their perches and on to the floor of the cave. They would die if they were not rescued. When the mother

Female bats and their young live in groups called nursery colonies. The baby clings to its mother's fur as she flies about.

returns from feeding, she picks up her own baby from the floor.

By autumn, the young bats can fly and feed themselves. Males, females, and young migrate back to their winter home. In places where suitable winter caves are scarce, summer and winter homes may be hundreds of kilometres apart.

Nomads with their Herds

Nowadays, most people have one home in which they live all year round. Not long ago, however, many people in different parts of the world used to have more than one home. Their homes were often hundreds of kilometres apart. People who spent their lives wandering from one home to the next were called nomads. A few groups of people still live like this today, and we will look at three of them.

Nomads are dependent on herds of animals such as goats, sheep, cattle, camels, and reindeer. They milk the animals, sometimes drink their blood, and kill them for their meat and skins. Herds of animals are always on the move, searching for food and water. Nomads follow their herds as they migrate from one season's home to the next. This is why the people are nomads. They have to lead their herds to places where water and food is available.

LAPLANDERS

Laplanders (or Lapps) live with herds of reindeer in Lapland. Lapland is a region of northern Norway, Sweden, and the Kola peninsula. In summer, the Lapps live with their reindeer along the coast of the Arctic Ocean, right at the very northern edge of Lapland. Here the reindeer feed on mosses and lichens.

At the end of September and the beginning of October, the reindeer herds begin to move southwards. The Lapps follow their animals. Some groups travel 400 km or more to winter homes in the mountains and forests inland. Here they are sheltered from the strong cold winds that blow at this time in the north. Also, there is plenty of food for the

Reindeer are nomads, therefore Lapps must be also. They follow their herds in summer as far as the coast of the Arctic Ocean.

reindeer among the trees. In April the Lapps and their herds head back to their summer homes on the northern coast. Their journey takes ten or twelve days. Some of the migration routes followed by the Laplanders are 400 years old.

BEDOUIN

Bedouin live in the hot deserts of the Arabian peninsula, northern Africa, and parts of Syria and Jordan. They live with herds which contain both sheep and camels. There is very little vegetation in deserts. This means that the nomads must forever follow their herds as they wander in search of somewhere to graze.

Some Bedouin tribes wander through areas as large as 55,000 square kilometres. Others travel round in huge circles about 240 km across. The Bedouin and their animals know where all the water holes are in this area, and where best to find green plants. The nomads travel on horseback, and live in tents.

During the hot, dry summers from June to October, the herds collect around water holes. Here there is always some greenery for them to eat. The Bedouin hope that their animals do not eat all the food before the beginning of the wet season, when fresh food will grow.

They leave the watering holes, along with their herds, at the beginning of November. They then spend the rainy season migrating with their herds, from one place where it has just rained to the next. This means that there is always fresh greenery for the animals to eat. By the beginning of the dry season, the Bedouin and their herds have to make sure that they are near the water holes again.

FULANI

The Fulani live on the savanna grasslands, just south of the Sahara desert, in north-western Africa. Their herds consist of cattle. The Fulani and their cattle have one home in the dry season, and another home in the wet season.

At the peak of the wet season, in August and September, many Fulani families and their animals gather and live together. This is the only time of the year when there is enough food in one place to feed a large number of cattle. At the beginning of the dry season all the people with their herds begin to migrate south, where water and green vegetation are still available.

However, once the ground begins to dry, and grass for the cows becomes more and more scarce, the people gradually have to split up. Eventually each family, with its own herd, is travelling alone on separate routes. Some families end up nearly 200 km from their northern homes.

When the wet season begins in April the families begin to head north again. If they stayed in the south, they and their cows would be attacked and bitten by a type of fly known as tsetse fly. Tsetse flies carry diseases such as 'sleeping sickness'. This disease can kill both cows and people. The Fulani travel north until they are safe from the tsetse flies. As the rain falls and the grass grows, the families gradually reunite, and hear about each others' adventures during the dry season.

Bedouin spend summer at oases. In the winter season they must migrate with their herds of sheep and camels, following the rains.

5 Long-Distance Migrations

So far, none of the animals we have looked at have migrated very great distances. We have looked at chimpanzees migrating a few kilometres between their wet season and dry season homes, and lemmings racing from one mountain top to another. We have also looked at beavers building new lodges and dams up to 10 km away, and bats migrating up to a few hundred kilometres between their summer and winter homes.

Now it is time to look at the real stars among mammal migrants. Some, like the caribou, migrate between summer and winter homes as much as 1,000 km apart. Others, like the tree bats, migrate at least 1,200 km every year. We shall also be looking at the magnificent herds of migrating wildebeest and zebra. These animals migrate thousands of kilometres across the great plains of Africa. However, let us start by looking at caribou.

Caribou of the Tundra

The caribou is a type of reindeer. Caribou live in an area of the world called the Arctic Circle. The Arctic Circle is a big area of land and sea around the North Pole. It includes

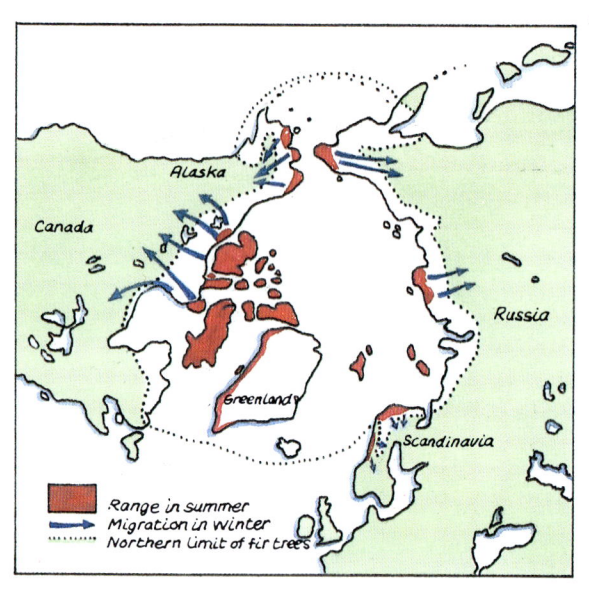

Some caribou spend summer on the shores of the Arctic Ocean. In winter they travel hundreds of kilometres south. There they will seek shelter in the fir forests from the icy winds.

parts of Canada, Alaska, Russia, and Scandinavia. The weather in the Arctic Circle is extremely cold. There is snow on the ground throughout most of the year, and even the summers are quite cold. The vegetation in the Arctic Circle is called 'tundra', just like the vegetation on the tops of mountains.

In summertime, the caribou live on the tundra. They make their winter homes in the great forests of fir trees that grow to the south of the tundra. To live in these two homes, some caribou have to migrate over

1,000 kilometres every year. A few travel twice as far.

The fir forest is a perfect winter home for the caribou. It is much warmer in the forests than on the tundra, and the trees shelter the animals from the icy north winds. Even here the ground is still covered with snow. The snow is light and fluffy, though, and the caribou can easily scrape it aside with their hooves. They dig holes in the snow so that they can get at the mosses and lichens which grow beneath. These are the caribou's main food.

The caribou leave their winter homes in the forest in February. They set off northwards through the snowy forests. They may have to migrate hundreds of kilometres before they reach the place where the forest dies out and the tundra begins. This place is called the 'tree line'. The caribou reach the tree line during the first week of May.

All winter, the caribou have been scattered through the forest in groups of less than 100. When they reach the tree line, these scattered groups gather together to form huge herds. Some herds contain as many as 100,000 caribou. The massive herds carry on migrating northwards. Female caribou always migrate at a much faster rate than the males. The males and younger caribou soon start to lag behind the impatient females. As the females increase their lead and the males lag

Females with their young cross Alaska's icy Kongakut River. The calves are almost ready to begin migrating for up to 1,000 kilometres.

further and further behind, the herd gets longer and longer. Some herds thin out to a length of 300 km and take several weeks to pass one point.

The Safety of the Calving Grounds

You may be wondering why the female caribou are in such a great hurry. They are hurrying to reach a safe place before their babies are born in June. Baby caribou are called calves. For a mother and her calf, the biggest enemies are wolves. The wolves which roam the icy tundra often prey on baby caribou.

Caribou are the only deer in which both the males and the females have big antlers. Sometimes, the females have to use their antlers to fight off wolves which attack their calves. While the calves are very young, though, the females try to avoid wolves altogether.

The females are very clever. They know certain places on the tundra where wolves are rare. Most of these places are on rugged highlands where the weather is very bitter. The females give birth to their calves in these highlands. The places where they give birth are called 'calving grounds'. Some females give birth on the very same calving ground on which they themselves were born.

In some areas, the nearest calving grounds may be 500 km north of the tree line. The pregnant females have only three weeks at the most to reach them. Heads down, they trudge on steadily northwards. On reaching the calving grounds and safety, the females give birth. The new-born

Females migrate swifter than males, racing to a safe place to give birth. Within three hours of being born this calf could outrun a man.

Once back in the fir forests the males become aggressive. These two large bulls are getting ready to fight because a female is near.

calves are strong enough to run with the herd in just a couple of hours. They feed on their mothers' milk and grow rapidly. By July, they are feeding themselves on mosses and lichens.

As soon as the young can fend for themselves, the herd moves on to lower ground. They may travel another 200 km to parts of the tundra where the food is much greener and more plentiful.

In August the caribou herds split up and start to migrate southwards to their winter homes. They travel in groups of two or three. They can migrate at a faster rate than they did through the snows of spring. Some groups migrate as many as 60 km a day. In September, the fat and healthy caribou arrive back at the treeline.

At the treeline, the caribou form herds again. The males start to get very excited and aggressive. The sound of clashing antlers can be heard ringing through the forest as the males fight over the females.

This is the mating season. The mating season produces the calves that will be born the following June. Once the mating is over, the herds migrate into the forests and on to their winter homes.

Tree Bats

In Chapter 4 we looked at bats which live in colonies. However, not all bats live in colonies. Tree bats

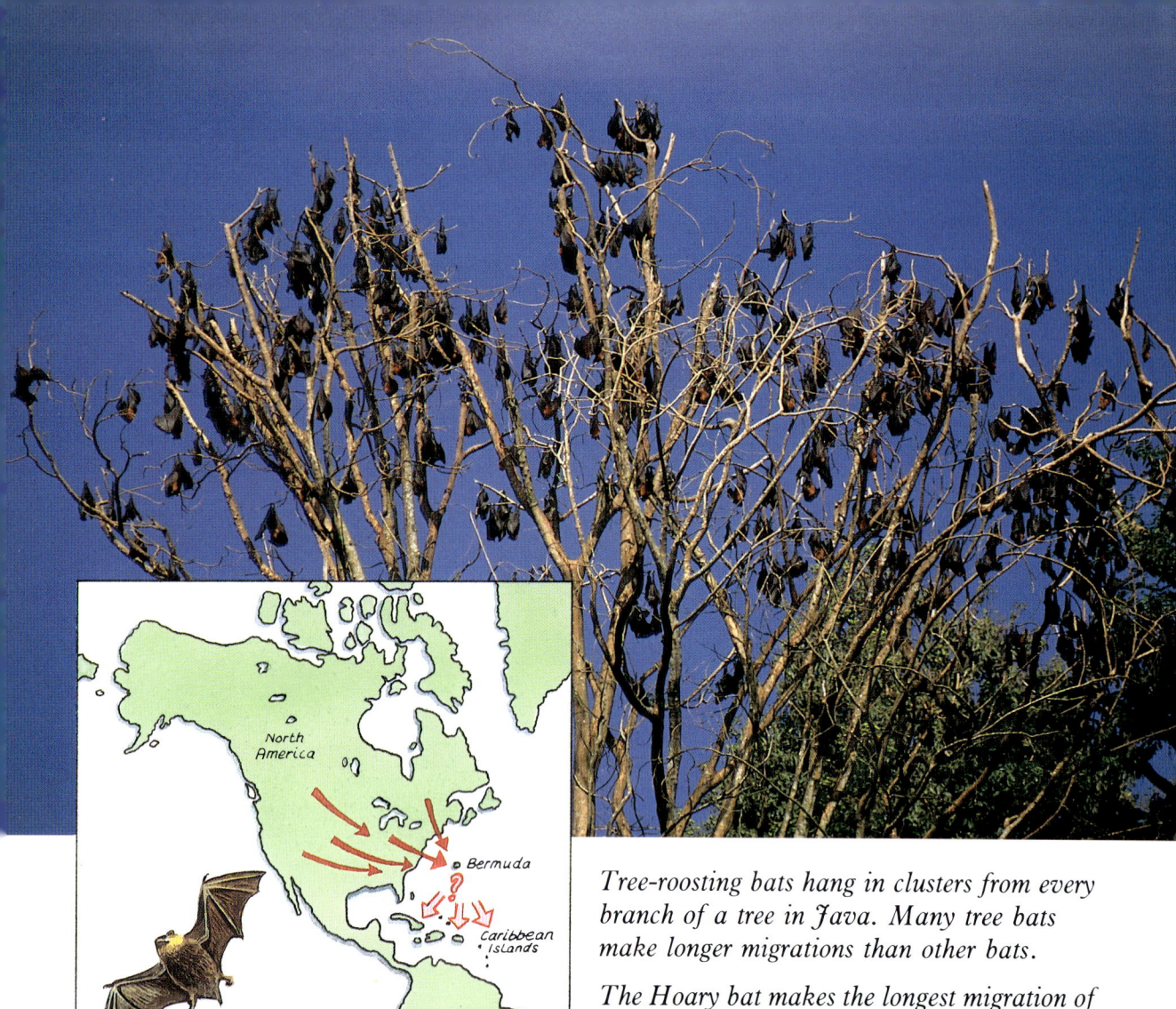

Tree-roosting bats hang in clusters from every branch of a tree in Java. Many tree bats make longer migrations than other bats.

The Hoary bat makes the longest migration of all. From North America it flies across the sea to Bermuda – then disappears!

spend most of their lives living alone. During the day they sleep in trees. They either hang from branches or squeeze themselves into holes in the tree trunk. Tree bats perform the longest migrations of all bats.

Tree bats of North America spend the summer hanging in trees in the great northern forests. During the summer the females give birth. Unlike cave bats, tree bats often give birth to twins.

In autumn, all the tree bats set off to their winter homes. However, exactly where they go to is a bit of a mystery. Tree bats are hardly ever seen in winter. However, we do know that one type of tree bat flies at least as far as Bermuda. This is the 'Hoary bat'.

Bermuda is an island in the Atlantic Ocean, off the coast of North America. To reach the island the Hoary bat has to fly non-stop over water for a distance of at least 1,200 km. The bats do not seem to stay in Bermuda, though. Perhaps they are just resting on their way to winter homes in the Caribbean Islands or South America. In spring, Hoary bats appear in Bermuda once again. Perhaps these are stopping off on their return migration.

Wildebeest and Zebra

In eastern central Africa are huge areas of grassland. Here live lions, cheetahs, leopards, giraffes, rhinoceroses, and many more magnificent animals. Most spectacular of all, though, are the migrating herds of wildebeest and zebra. The wildebeest or gnu is a type of antelope with thin legs and a head which looks far too big for its body. Thousands of wildebeest and zebra migrate together in huge herds between their dry season and wet season home ranges.

Wildebeest and zebra make their dry season homes around Lake Victoria. Here the huge herds graze on the ragged, scrubby woodlands

Thin, dry grass grows beside the waterhole. But soon the rumble of distant thunder will set these African zebra migrating again.

that lie on the edge of the grassy plains. In these scrubby woodlands there is always some old but green vegetation for the animals to eat. In December the first storms of the wet season occur. After the storm, the first blades of fresh grass begin to grow on the plains.

The fresh grass grows only in the places where there are storms. The wildebeest and zebra migrate to the places where it has just rained, to feed on the fresh vegetation. Often the migrant herds will travel to a storm that is raging up to 100 km away. They spend the wet season criss-crossing the plains, migrating from one storm to the next.

But, you may be asking yourself, how do the herds know where the rains are falling? The wildebeest and zebra listen carefully to the sound of distant thunder. When they are certain they know which direction the thunder is coming from, they set off towards it. The animals can also observe the clouds! The clouds also give them clues about where the rain is falling.

Crossing Rivers

Sometimes the migrants have to cross wide rivers. Often, the rivers are in flood with the water from rains falling many miles away. The older members of the herd know all the best crossing places. Some of the older animals may have been roaming the plains for thirty

Exhausted by their battle against the river current, a herd of wildebeest struggle up the slippery banks of the Mara in Tanzania.

years. However, crossing the fast-flowing rivers is still not easy for the migrating herd.

The animals have to be strong enough to battle against the current. Even at the safest crossing places, many animals fail to reach the other side. Some, especially the old or sickly, die of exhaustion in the water. Many calves are caught up in the strong currents. Wide-eyed with fear, and braying helplessly, they are swept further and further away from their mothers.

Some do not even manage to get down into the water safely. The river banks are often steep and slippery. There is a tremendous crush as the thousands of animals try to clamber down. The ones at the front are pushed forward by those behind. Many of them slip, breaking legs and sometimes even their necks. Hundreds can be lost at a single crossing.

In June, when the herds have fed well for four or five months, the plains dry out. This is the beginning of the dry season. The herds start to migrate north-westwards, back to Lake Victoria and their dry season homes.

Female wildebeest and zebra do not have special calving grounds like the caribou of Canada. They give birth in December and January,

Despite river crossings, and a midday rest in the shade, wildebeest herds have been known to travel up to 50 kilometres in a day.

right at the beginning of the wet season. At this time there is plenty of fresh food for the young animals to eat. The mothers give birth while they are following the storms. The herd pauses only long enough for the new-born calves to find their feet. Within just a few hours, the young wildebeest or zebra has to be able to run fast enough to keep up with the rest of the herd.

Saiga

In the middle of Europe and Asia there are vast areas of grassland. These grasslands are known as the 'steppes'. The weather in the steppes is very harsh. Although the summers are nearly as hot as those in the grasslands of Africa, the winters are extremely cold. The ground becomes covered with snow and ice and in many places the grass is buried deeply.

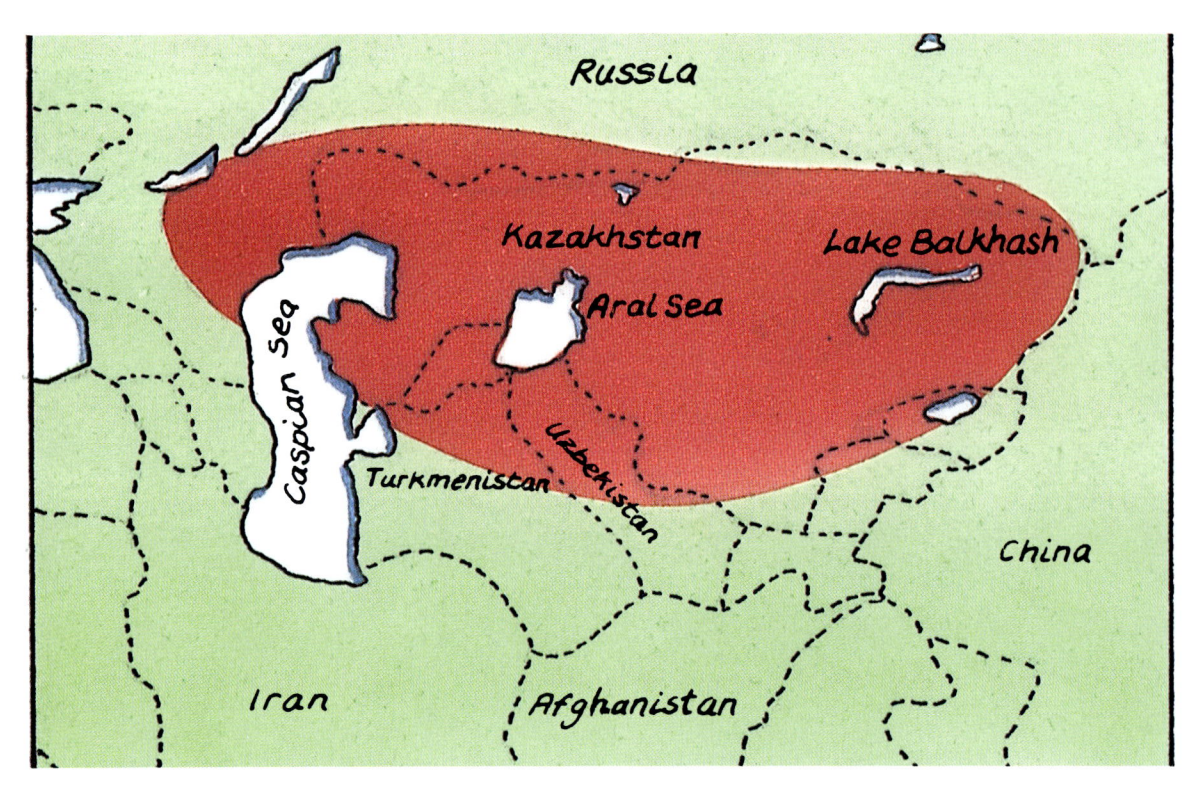

Until recently, many large animals used to live and migrate on the steppes. At one time there were huge herds of European bison. Herds of wild horses, known as 'Przewalski's horse' used to gallop across the desolate plains. Most of these large animals have been killed off. People killed the animals for food, or to make room on the land for their farms. Now, the only large animal still living and migrating on the steppes is the strange-looking Saiga.

Saiga give birth near the Caspian Sea. During the rest of the year they roam a territory covering seven countries of central Asia.

The saiga looks like a cross between a sheep, a goat, and an antelope. It has a long neck and very big, bulbous nostrils.

Just like caribou, saiga have special calving grounds. The females give birth each year in spring. The calving grounds are near the Caspian Sea. The saiga have to migrate about 300 km to reach them. Some saiga migrate in quite small groups. Others migrate in huge herds containing up to 100,000.

The migrating saiga form long columns as they trudge through the snow. Some of these columns are over a kilometre wide. If the weather

The saiga is not a handsome animal, but its migrations are spectacular. It moves in vast herds, and for short distances can run at 80 kilometres per hour.

is very bad, the migrants make only very slow progress. Sometimes the saiga have to battle their way through storms and blizzards. However, usually it takes the migrants about two weeks to reach the calving grounds. Here the females give birth to their young.

As soon as the young saiga can keep up with their mothers, the herd sets off back to its summer home. Just like the wildebeest in Africa, they criss-cross the plains in search of food and water. In August they begin to wander eastwards back towards the Caspian Sea. Then, with the first snow in November, they set off southwards to their winter feeding grounds.

The saiga spend the winter in these feeding grounds, searching for places where the snow is thin enough to be scraped aside. Just like caribou, saiga feed on the grasses that are buried beneath the snow. In spring they start the long, hard migration back to the calving grounds near the Caspian Sea.

American Bison

The bison has not survived as well as the saiga. For thousands of years these magnificent creatures lived on the great grassy plains in the middle of North America. Their only enemies were wolves and the various tribes of American Indians. The American Indians hunted the bison for food and skins.

The bison thrived. When the first Europeans arrived in America, a few hundred years ago, there were about 60 million bison. They lived in an

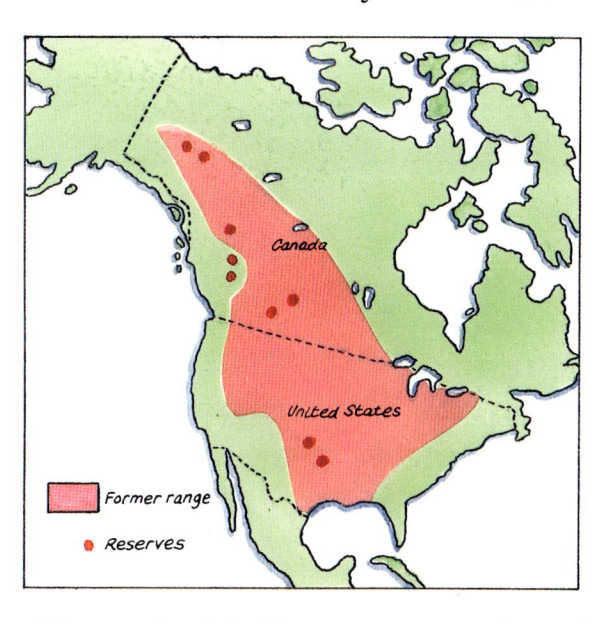

Bison used to inhabit an enormous territory of North America. Sadly, they live now only on a few reservations, and can no longer migrate very far.

43

Bison are no longer seen in herds numbering hundreds of thousands. This family grazes in Yellowstone National Park.

area that stretched from southern Canada to northern Mexico. Just like the saiga on the steppes of Europe and Asia, the bison used to migrate in huge herds across the plains. They migrated from summer to winter homes and back again. Just like wildebeest, there was no real pattern to their movements. Each year they would travel up to a thousand kilometres as they crisscrossed the American prairies.

Bison did not like climbing hills. Whenever they could, they would migrate along valleys. The men who built America's railways constantly found themselves following the bison trails.

The earliest Europeans were amazed at the size of the migrant herds. A single herd could contain millions, and cover more than a hundred square kilometres. In 1871, a herd 80 km long and 40 km wide was seen crossing the Arkansas River!

The Europeans who settled in North America ruthlessly slaughtered the bison. In the years from 1870 to 1875, over 12 million bison were shot. Many were killed just so that people could eat the tongue. The rest of the animal was left to rot. By 1880 there were no herds left in the area south of the Arkansas River. Nine years later there were only 1,091 bison left alive.

Almost too late, reservations were set up for the bison to live in. This gentle giant among migrants soon became a protected species. Now there are about 30,000 bison scattered all over North America. However, they cannot migrate from their reservations. The magnificent sight of the vast migrating herds has gone forever.

Glossary

Arctic/Arctic Circle The Arctic is the whole area of the globe lying to the north of 66 degrees north latitude. The Arctic Circle is the line drawn on a map or globe which marks this boundary.

colony A large number of animals such as bats, rabbits etc. which live together in a fixed home.

fixed home The home of certain animals, for example squirrels and beavers, to which they return each night for warmth and shelter. Many mammals do not have such homes.

grassland Land on which grass is the main vegetation, like American prairie or East African plains.

herd A large number of wandering mammals (such as caribou, zebra, etc) living together as a group.

hibernation The state similar to a deep sleep in which various animals including some mammals spend the winter months.

home range The area in which wanderers move about.

mammal All creatures whose young feed on milk from the mother's body.

mating A female animal joining with a male animal to produce young. All mammals are born from their parents mating.

migrant/migrate/migration The habit of moving from one habitat to another (usually in search of food) is called *migration*. An animal that *migrates* is a *migrant*.

nomads Groups of people who wander from place to place to find the best grazing places for their herds.

north The direction a compass needle points. Most maps are drawn so that the northernmost part is at the top.

North Pole The northernmost point of the earth. It is surrounded by ocean covered with permanent ice.

predator An animal which hunts and kills other animals for food.

south The direction opposite to north.

treeline The furthest point north or south (or the highest altitude) at which it is possible for trees to grow.

tropics An area around the centre of the earth reaching $23\frac{1}{2}$ degrees either side of the equator. Within this band, about 5,500 km wide, the climate is very hot.

tundra A vast area lying south of the Arctic where no trees will grow on the frozen sub-soil. The word also describes the scant type of vegetation which grows there in summer, and above the treeline on mountains.

wanderers Animals which do not have a fixed home like a cave or den, but which wander about and sleep in a different place each day or night.

Bibliography

MIGRATION
Adult books which older children would enjoy

Baker, R.R., *The Mystery of Migration* (Macdonald).
Ricard, Matthieu, *The Mystery of Animal Migration* (Constable)

NATURAL HISTORY
Children's books containing some information on migration

Althea, *Mountain Homes* (C.U.P)
Clarkson, Ewan, *Beavers* (Wayland)
Feder, Jan, *The Life of a Rabbit* (Hutchinson)
Hughes, Jill, *Arctic Lands* (Hamish Hamilton)
Pratt, Paulette, *Animal Life* (Hodder)
Soper, Tony, *Discovering Animals* (BBC)
Stehli, G and Brohmer, P, *Mammals* (Burke Books)
Vevers, Gwynne, *Animal Homes* (Bodley Head)

Picture Sources

ARDEA: Yann Arthus-Bertram 21; Ian Beames 14, 23; G.K. Brown 33; Jean-Paul Ferrero 15; Kenneth W. Fink 8, 43 upper; Francois Gohier 20, 44; Martin N. Grosnick 16; Clem Haagner 6, 29, 39; Jack Swedberg 25; A. Warren 10.

Bruce Coleman: Helmut Albrecht 27; B and C Alexander 32; R.I.M. Campbell 22; Jeff Foott 12–13; Steven Kaufman 35, 36; John Shaw 37; Kim Taylor 7; Peter Ward 31; WWF/Eric Dragesco 17; Gunter Ziesler 11, cover and 40, 41.

Simon Girling Associates/Richard Hull: cover inset, 18–19, 28, 34, 38 lower, 42, 43 lower.

Wildlife Matters: 38 upper

ZEFA: E & P Bauer 30; K. Rohrich 9.

Index

A
Africa 22, 26, 28–9, 32, 33, 39
Alaska 34, 35
America, *see* North America; United States
American bison, *see* bison
antelope 39
Arabia 32
Arctic 31, 34, 45
Arkansas River 44
Asia 24, 41, 42
Atlantic Ocean 38
Australia 23

B
bat
  cave bats 9–10, 29–31
  fruit bats 10
  Hoary bat 33–4
  tree bats 37–9
  Vampire bat 10–11
bear, *see* Grizzly bear
beaver 24–5
Bedouin 32–3
Bermuda 38
birth
  caribou 36
  cave bats 29
  Grizzly bear 12
  saiga 43
  tree bats 38
  wildebeest 41
  zebra 41
bison 43–4
Britain 14

C
camel 33
Canada 6, 16, 34, 44, *see also* North America
Caribbean 38
caribou 6, 34–7
Caspian Sea 42, 43
cattle 33
cave bats 9–10
Central America 11
chimpanzee 26–8
colonies 11, 30, 45
cougar 9
coyote 9

E
echo-location by bats 10
elephant 26, 28–9
Europe 15, 23, 24, 41

F
family groups
  gorilla 22
  Grizzly bear 12
  humans 33
fixed homes 8–14, 45
  beaver 24–5
  Grey squirrel 8, 13–14
  mouse 8, 13
Fulani 33

G
gorilla 7, 21–2
Grey squirrel 8, 13–14
Grizzly bear 9, 12–13

H
herds and other large groups 45
  bat 10–11
  bison 44
  camel 32–3
  caribou 35
  cattle 33
  chimpanzee 26
  elephant 28
  Mountain sheep 16–17
  rabbit 23–4
  reindeer 31
  saiga 42
  Scandinavian lemming 18–20
  sheep 32–3
  wildebeest 39
  zebra 39
hibernation 12, 45
Hoary bat 6
home range 21, 26, 28, 45
horse 42
human migration
  Bedouin 32–3
  Fulani 33
  Lapps 31–2

J
Java 38
Jordan 32

K
Kenya 29
Kola peninsula 31
Kongakut River, Alaska 35

L
Lake Victoria 39, 41
Lapland 31
Lapps 31–2
lemming, *see* Scandinavian lemming

M
Mara River, Tanzania 40
Mexico 44
migration
  alone 6, 29
  at night 7, 19
  definition of 2, 6, 45
  in herds 6, *see also* herds

Mountain sheep 16–17
mouse 8, 13
Mount Kenya 29
muskrat 15–16

N
nomads 31–3, 45
North America 6, 9, 12, 15, 24, 38, 43, *see also* Canada; United States
North Pole 34, 45
Norway 11, 31
nursery colony 30

P
predators of mammals 45
　chimpanzee 27
　fox 16, 18, 25
　hawk 16
　humans 31, 42, 43, 44
　owl 16, 18
　stoat 16
　tsetse fly 33
　Vampire bat 10–11
　wolf 16, 25, 36, 43

Przewalski's horse 42

R
rabbit 23–4
reindeer 31
Russia 34
Rwanda 22

S
Sahara Desert 33
saiga 41–3
Scandinavia 34, *see also* Lapland, Norway, Sweden
Scandinavian lemming 7, 18–20
sheep 33, *see also* Mountain sheep
South America 11, 38
squirrel, *see* Grey squirrel
Sweden 18, 31
Syria 32

T
Tanzania 40

U
United States 14, *see also* North America

V
Vampire bat 10–11

W
wanderers 45
　bison 44
　gorilla 7, 22
　wildebeest 40
　zebra 40
wild cat 9
wild dog 9
wildebeest 39–41

Y
Yellowstone National Park, Wyoming 44

Z
zebra 39–41